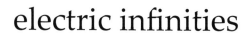

electric infinities

electric infinities

Library of Congress Control Number: 2022945299

ISBN: 978-1-955602-10-5 (paperback)

Published in the United States of America

Published by Variant Literature Inc
www.variantlit.com

Cover Design by Ashley Cline

table of contents

the companion mixtape

electric
infinities

playing at an apocalypse near you

Why do the birds go on singing? / Why do the stars glow above?
Don't they know it's the end of the world?

[Skeeter Davis, 1962]

checklist for the end of the world

- ☐ a healthy snack
- ☐ make it honeydew
- ☐ & don't forget money,
    to burn: literally —
    there will be so much

- ☐ burning, & this is
- ☐ something
    that you are not prepared for —
    will never be prepared for —
    but you will learn to see the

- ☐ ash as
- ☐ something beautiful, if not
- ☐ a heaviness,
    that you cannot place / like

- ☐ rock sherbet, or
- ☐ star signs, or
- ☐ a sneaking suspicion
    that this will all make sense, one day —

- ☐ the audacity of hope
    is funny like that; so funny, in fact,
    that you don't forget to laugh —
    even though the world is ending —
    even though you have but

- ☐ one body, to forgive.

the way the universe will end, scenario no. 1

by now you know that anything can be beautiful inside of a poem—

& so: you write yourself into one / & it's here that you think: *curb your gods*. it's here, that you think / *you've got your heart three ways, sweetie.*

& it's here: that you think of the bird / & how they can fly because they are hollow / know how their bones beneath feathers spiral like miniature

galaxies, pneumatized; or like sun-dried magicians / & it's here that you think of yourself / how your hollowness differs from that of the bird's—

how it lives in your body & holds you too close / how it makes you— — heavier, somehow; unfit for flight / but by now you have learned to stop

wishing yourself a ghost / & so: you wish to be something more sturdy, more solid, instead / like a nice piece of furniture, or the only thing that

survives the fire because, by now / you are so tired of spilling into your own hands, & so: you pluck them from your wrists / & let your body fall

to the floor, freely & with grace—& it's then / that you plant your hands in the garden, palms up / so that they might always catch the sun. & it's

there that a boy will bloom come spring / & know that he will be blue; know that he will be blue & filthy / & happy to see you—& just know:

you will name him after everything that you could never be.

everyone i know is disappearing

not literally, though maybe. it depends on how you weigh a memory.
do you turn it over in your hands? palm it smooth as birth? or do you bring

it to your mouth, rest its heft against your cheek & let it melt on the tongue?
they say nostalgia causes cancer. artificial sweetness gulped down hot & whole,

but you remember like you don't mind. say you'd rather *kick it clean, anyway.*
whatever that means. say *imagine the ostrich* — & so, i do — i imagine being in love

with myself in a way that cannot be mistaken for cowardice; in a way that does
not end in tributaries or tributes, or in mute teeth & mixtapes left unlistened to —

& i do not know this girl, but i'd like to. she seems like someone who would not
click on the article *how to read the doomsday clock* — because she does not need to

split time open & count its rings; because she did not read *how to rename a place,*
& so, she sings everywhere a pop song, instead — the kitchen. *cut to the feeling* blue.

the bedroom. *touch & go* disco. & this patience? learned from gladys. so that her
slanted house blushes gladiolus in the night; softens pelvis into garden dirt,

& suddenly — petals.

no pulp, or a lesson in permeance

& suddenly the summer heat blushes mango ripe / buries her hurricane
stone in my throat / & this is a body pressed: reserve the juice—

pour it into the cheek of another & call it *magnolia tree* / call it *150 hands
at your back* / i need a witness for all these miracles—

the dogwoods dressed in dappled fever / & you, making a pupil of my tongue
like i said: *miracles* / like i said—

i scatter hair everywhere i go, i will haunt these lemon groves sour / so save
the rinds & divide the flesh / make a pulpit out of all of this—

this is my body: now eat.

[field note from the end of the world:

when honeybee one asked honeybee two, "do you ever wanna fuck around & fall in love?" honeybee two said, "yes, i think about death—but that is different"]

portrait of death as the mean girl you once loved

there are several steps to gutting a fish; "bleeding out" is perhaps the most important. a fish that is caught & kept, but not properly bled out, will most likely still be alive while on the cutting board. not only will this be messy—for you—but these final moments of immense stress—as the fish struggles against death—burns her flesh, resulting in a fillet that tastes acidic—bitter, even.

she is pretty because she is mean, or maybe: she is mean
because she is pretty—it is hard to say, for sure. just as it
is hard to know exactly when

you first learned what quick work this world makes of soft
things which means *pink* things which means *you* things—
& she is the one

who first told you that *it's gut or be gutted*—with traceable
tongue—as she stood upon the shoulders of that august &
set her hip in defiance & aqualung—

still pretty, as she filleted your summer
along the bone.

a series of questions & answers, in no particular order

how many centimeters are in a mile? & can i substitute inches for—

5 peaches—sliced—about 3 cups; then mix with 3/4 cup granulated
sugar & 1/4 teaspoon of salt. for best results—

is *doomsday* one word? or two—

& yes, there is at least one fig wasp, dead; something about *you gotta
crack a few eggs to make an omelette*, or—

whatever god said to eve in the garden, gossiped communion—

*in barbecue sauce & the trick is you gotta cook 'em low-n-slow
if you want your ribs to fall off the bone, tender*—

translation: walk away human.

the way the universe will end, scenario no. 2

i will place my head on the table / & i will simply leave it
there, forever / perhaps, one day, a flower will grow—
perhaps, perhaps, perhaps, perhaps.

the way the universe will end, scenario no. 3

some animals are beginning to shape-shift their bodies / & we let them
we have run out of questions to ask / & even if that were true
who's listening, anyway

to the dagger mouth moth returning to silk / to the fen rabbits sleeping
in their thrifted gowns / watch now, how our dusted brothers dress
themselves in honeydewed furs

& curve their bones back into scripture / watch: how they beg their hides
into grace—stop asking me about the future / i do not see myself
there, instead

ask me about janis ian & the way she sings the blues / watch with me
now / how the needle skates, & she whispers: *i know how it ends
& yes, it is true—*

this universe will balloon herself lonely & cold, one day / just like every
woman carved into my ribs has done before / so ask me, instead
about the late-afternoon sun

so that i may tell you all the ways in which / she tricks the water ever more
blue / & ask me, instead, about how she coaxes the gold from the
cheeks of this coast

so that i might tell you how she was king all along / so that i might tell you
how i wish to be gutted with hands / far more steady than mine
until

there are no more electric infinities / until the horse flies circle overhead
& the horse flies buzz—they never stop buzzing—
& death unquiets.

[field note from the end of the world:

she thinks "i want to be happy," then blows; the nature of the birthday wish,
is such, that it must always end in smoke]

a scientifically accurate poem

did you know that the moon is drifting away from the earth at about
four centimeters a year

& that four centimeters is roughly the same size as three honeybees
stacked one on top of the other

& if one hundred & twenty-nine thousand nine hundred & twenty-six
honeybees stood head upon wing,

they would reach the top of the cumbre vieja volcano, which nests in the
canary islands;

which erupted on september nineteenth; which buried six beehives in ash
for no less than fifty days—

but the honeybees survived, five out of six hives to be exact, which the
locals called *the sweetest miracle*;

like finding carbon inside of a two-point-billion-year-old ruby, like fitting
every planet in our solar system between

the moon & earth—& like earth with all her honeybees softly singing:
death ain't nothin' but honey made different.

portrait with my mother's hands

my mother says *there are no shortcuts through girlhood,* & so:
i dream myself loved, instead. which is the next best thing, i figure,

because *loneliness cannot touch what it cannot see.* & sometimes
i sing the yellow off a canary just to bring the color back to earth, just

to hold a toothless sun in the palm of my right hand. & it does not
bite. it does not burn. & it does not ask me for my ABC's, which is just

a currency, after all—another way of getting me to spell out *lonely* or
blue or *delaware,* all the things i know my favorite river to be; & all the

things i know which best describe the day i was born. when my mother
said: *you will not be a virgo!* & so, i am not. because my mother willed me

into being. because my mother pulled me from the mud. because my
mother pushed me through wildness, honey-fanged & fallow—

& still, the stars' protests echo on.

the way the universe will end, scenario no. 4

1. they say it started with a double exposure, a planet there then gone. 2. when we say we want a creation story what we mean is we want a myth that we can believe in. 3. so she hands you the knife. she doesn't tell you how the fish dies; just knows. 4. that the world is shrinking, which is different than becoming small. 5. because. 6. this isn't a metaphor. 7. when we say that we are wounded what we mean is that, sometimes, honeybees become canaries. 8. what we mean is: birthday candle; then smoke, then smoke. 9. *so draw your dead, & draw your living.* 10. *now tell me who smiles more?* you said, you said —

the way the universe will end, scenario no. 5

not with a bang / nor a whimper / or with a whisper of a bird in flight / but rather / with a text: one that will read / *now that i know that you are not dead, look at this sky* / & look at the sky we will / we will / we will / we will / we will / we will.

...until there is nothing left

but the loneliness pruned from my chest,
but the garden gone feral; but the red oaks,
        inverted; & the flowers grown carnivorous;
but the cool, damp earth staining your teeth,
but the dandelion wine down your chin,
but the himalayas made into pebbles
        & scattered & kansas crying dust in the wind;
but our fears undressing in pairs by the bedside,
but our tongues tied off in tulle & prayer,
but the old gods made human, brought in from
        the cold, & the dog stars left chasing their tails;
but skeeter davis singing—& i really mean singing—
        don't they know it's the end of the world?

        & until then: we'll slow dance. like nothing else
        is worth doing; we'll slow dance in/to

                                the end.

epilogue

after sputnik 2 returns to earth

at 5:30 a.m. on November 3, 1957, Laika — a stray dog found on the streets of Moscow; an even-tempered & pup-less husky-spitz mix — was sent into space aboard Sputnik 2 with one meal & a seven-day oxygen supply. in the end, she would not need either. during the rigorous launch, with G-forces reaching five times that of normal gravity, the heat shield of her capsule was lost; while Laika became the first living creature in space — & circled the earth in about 103 minutes — she died shortly after liftoff due to the extreme heat inside the capsule. Sputnik 2 continued its orbit for five months, however, circling the earth 2,570 times...

when they unspool you from the ocean / & untangle you from
that comet come & gone / you become a gilded thing in gentle

gold; an alchemy that does not ache / for once, an endeavor of
man that does not end in death / because you are the endeavor,

love; a letter to infinity / a story i write over & over & over—
again / i am choosing you fireproof.

portrait of the body as a map labeled terra incognita

you ask me for my favorite flower, & i tell you that
i prefer the kind with roots; the ones that do not start

or end with death; the daisies or the hyacinths that do
not make a god of simple hands; those are the ones that

i like best. because we are clumsy creatures, in the end;
we reach for stars & we pull down bodies; we reach for

warmth & we dig up gardens, whole, instead; what i'm
trying to say, is: the wildflowers have bloomed, & i

wish to join them—oh, the wildness i'd grow,
just to see you dressed in green.

in lieu of singing "happy birthday"

sing me gold & sing me blue; sing me back into the mud & clay / & then: carve into me your initials; alphabet like origin story, bone deep / an artist by osmosis—true, i am much too tenderhearted for your end of the worlds / & when i ask for fire, what i mean is singe my fingers back into forests, whole / & they will give their thanks in feathered things & fragile sap / & when you give me an open flame / make it a gift, instead—true, i no longer believe in wishes / but i believe that we should still eat this cake / *'cause you can always spare the sugar through the smoke, my love* / isn't that what your mother always said? / *you can always spare the sugar* / true.

author's : notes & acknowledgments

the text found before the poem "portrait of death as the mean girl you once loved" is an amalgamation of information found in the articles: "How to Fillet a Fish" [wikiHow] & "Why Bleeding Fish is So Important [Sushi Everyday].

the line *some animals are beginning to shape-shift their bodies* found in the poem, "the way the universe will end, scenario no. 3," is taken from a tweet posted by NPR on Sept. 9, 2021 (& links to the article: "Climate Change Is Making Some Species Of Animals Shape-Shift" written by Jonathan Franklin). i misread the tweet originally, however, & thought it said: "some animals are begging to shapeshift their bodies," which i found relatable.

"a scientifically accurate poem" pulls from the articles: "The Moon Is Leaving Us" by Marina Karen [The Atlantic; Sept. 30, 2021], "Beekeepers discover thousands of bees that survived 50 days of volcanic ash on La Palma" [Eminetra. co.uk; Nov. 11, 2021] & "Ancient Traces of Life Discovered Encased in a 2.5 Billion-Year-Old Ruby" written by the University of Waterloo [SciTechDaily; Oct. 24, 2021]. the math cited, which is the author's, could be wrong.

written by composer Arthur Kent & lyricist Sylvia Dee, & recorded by Skeeter Davis in June of 1962, "The End of the World" is the first—& to date— only song to crack the Top 10 on all four *Billboard* charts; the scholarly source, Wikipedia, describes it as "a sad song."

the text found before the poem, "after sputnik 2 returns to earth," was constructed piecemeal from the article: "The Sad, Sad Story of Laika, the Space Dog, and Her One-Way Trip into Orbit" written by Alice George for *Smithsonian Magazine* [April 11, 2018]; the story is just as sad in summary, in my opinion.

***

"the way the universe will end, scenario no. 1," "everyone i know is disappearing" and "no pulp, or a lesson in permeance" were first published in *Olney Magazine* • "the way the universe will end, scenario no. 3" appears in the anthology *Suicid(al)iens (Gutslut Press)* • "portrait with my mother's hands" was published in *Mausoleum Press* (Issue 03: Nebula) • "…until there is nothing left" first appeared in *celestite poetry* (issue 4) • "in lieu of singing 'happy birthday'" appears in *The Hellebore* (Issue 10) • "portrait of the body as a map labeled terra incognita" was published in *Rough Cut Press* (Issue 35)

***

with my first acknowledgments page, i wrote that writing is a lonely thing, inherently so. & while i still believe that to be true, how lucky am i that the list keeps growing, year after year—

to the readers & editors, journals & mags who have given me their time (a finite thing), & my poems space (which is not as infinite as we believe): thank you—

to *Variant Lit*, for embracing my many apocalypses: thank you—

to Tyler Pufpaff, who is the kind of editor a silly little poet like me could only ever dream of working with, thank you: for your guidance, your kindness, & your patience. i may have occasionally second-guessed this collection, but you never did—

to Katrina Smolinsky, Adam Gianforcaro, Madeleine Corley, & Elizabeth Deanna Morris Lakes: thank you, thank you, thank you, thank you. we all have such busy little lives, & yet you made time for this collection. & oh, how generous you were—

to Gardner Dorton & Josie Hegarty, for reading every last iteration of these poems, & then reading them again & again: thank you, thank you—

to Joe Penn: i am so thankful for all this poetry that we've got—

to James: thank you for the sandwiches, & everything else, too—

& mom, for keeping the end-of-the-world far away: thank you.

about the author

An avid introvert, full-time carbon-based life-form & aspiring himbo, Ashley Cline's poetry has appeared here, & also there. A two-time Pushcart nominee & Best of the Net 2020 finalist, she is also the author of: *& watch how easily the jaw sings of god* (Glass Poetry Press, 2021), *should the earth reclaim you* (Bone & Ink Press, 2023), *& cowabungaly yours at the end of the world* (Gutslut Press, 2023). Once, in the summer of 2019, she crowd-surfed an inflatable sword to Carly Rae Jepsen, and her best at all-you-can-eat sushi is 5 rolls in 11 minutes. Twitter: @the_Cline. Instagram: @ clineclinecline.